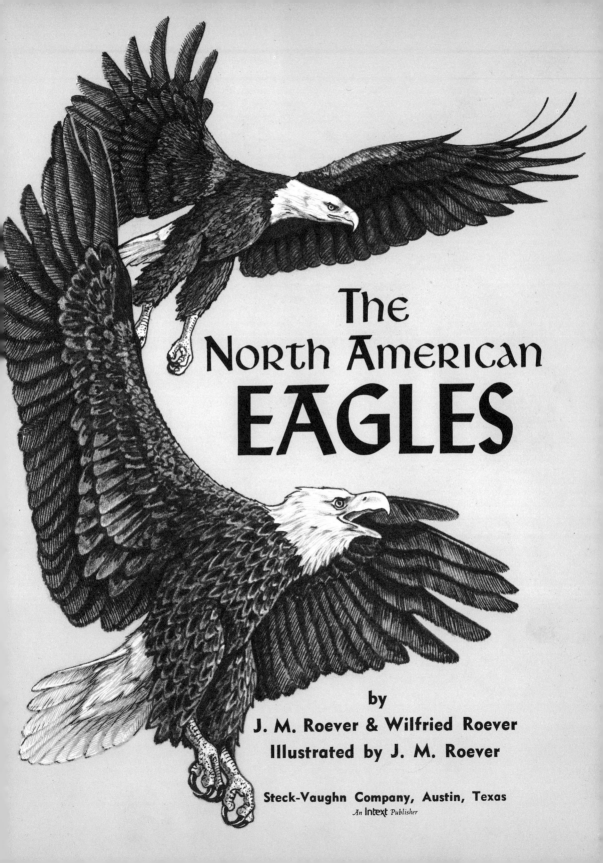

# The North American EAGLES

by
**J. M. Roever & Wilfried Roever**
**Illustrated by J. M. Roever**

**Steck-Vaughn Company, Austin, Texas**
*An* **Intext** *Publisher*

Golden Eagle

Library of Congress Cataloging in Publication Data

Roever, J        M
    The North American eagles.

    SUMMARY: Traces the importance of eagles in history and legend, describes
the characteristics, habits, and habitat of the bald and golden eagle, and explains
why their existence is threatened.

    1. Bald eagle—Juvenile literature. 2. Golden eagle—Juvenile literature. [1.
Eagles]
    I. Roever, Wilfried, joint author. II. Title.
QL696.A2R6        598.9'1        72-8994
ISBN 0-8114-7755-X

ISBN 0-8114-7755-X
Library of Congress Catalog Card Number 72-8994
Copyright © 1973 by J. M. Roever
All Rights Reserved
Printed and Bound in the United States of America

Bald Eagle

## The North American Eagles

With fierce eyes, regal appearance, magnificent wingspread, and great size, the bald eagle and golden eagle symbolize courage, wisdom, independence, strength, and vigilance.

Bird of Freedom, Master of All It Surveys, King of the Birds, Ruler of the Skies, Lord of the Air—these titles are often given to the North American eagles.

1

## "A" for Eagle

Thousands of years ago, Egyptian scholars used the profile of an eagle as a symbol in their hieroglyphs (hy-eh-ruh-glifs). To the religious Egyptians, the majestic eagle represented the free-soaring soul of man.

Neighboring Phoenicians (feh-nish-uhns) simplified the Egyptian picture writing into the first alphabet. The Egyptian eagle symbol became the lowercase letter "a." Can you see the eagle's curved beak, proud breast, and sweeping tail in the small letter "a"?

Beak

Breast

Tail

Egyptian Hieroglyph

2

## The Eagle in the Stars

Within the southern
portion of the Milky Way
in the summer sky, ancient
astrologers (uh-strol-uh-jerz)
saw the star shape of a
great flying bird.
They gave the group of
stars the Latin name Aquila
(ak-wih-luh), the eagle.

On a clear summer night
you can still locate Aquila's
constellation (kon-stuh-lay-shun).
The eagle's left shoulder is
adorned by Altair (awl-tay-ir),
"the flyer," one of the brightest
stars in the heavens.

Big Dipper

Polaris, the
North Star

Little Dipper

Draco, the Dragon

Cygnus, the
Swan

Lyra, the
Lyre

Sagitta, the Arrow

Delphinus,
the Dolphin

Aquila, the Eagle

Altair, "The Flyer"

The Constellation Aquila

**The Milky Way**

In August, Aquila can be located by finding
these familiar constellations. With this page
open, face south and gaze skyward. The constellations will appear overhead in this arrange-
ment.

# The Bald Eagle, Our National Emblem

Found nowhere else in the world except North America, the bald eagle is often called the American eagle.

In 1782 the Continental Congress adopted a design with a bald eagle as the Great Seal of the United States, and in 1789 Congress authorized it as our national emblem.

**Silver Dollar**

The image of a bald eagle has been used in our country on postage stamps; on paper money and many coins; on military insignias, medals, and flags; on many state seals and flags, and as a symbol for freedom, power, or merit.

EAGLE was the name of the Apollo 11 moon landing vehicle. On July 20, 1969, astronaut Neil Armstrong sent this message back to earth—"The EAGLE has landed!"

**Airmail Stamp**

More than any other bird's name, that of the eagle has been selected for streets, bridges, cities, towns, islands, lakes, rivers, and mountains.

## The Great Seal of the United States of America

The olive branch in the eagle's right foot represents peace. The 13 arrows in its left foot represent power. The 13 original colonies are indicated by the 13 red and white stripes on the breast shield. The banner shows the Latin motto, E Pluribus Unum, "Out of Many, One."

Use of the Great Seal is protected by law. It appears on some proclamations, the commissions of certain civil officers, and documents of international affairs.

**Congressional Medal of Honor (Army)**

**Eagle Badge of Merit (Boy Scouts of America)**

**Official Insignia of Apollo 11 Moon Mission**

## The Golden Eagle, Mexico's National Emblem

According to ancient legend, the Aztec Indians discovered their promised land in a valley in Mexico. There, as prophesied, they saw a great eagle perching upon a cactus plant and overpowering a serpent.

In 1821 the golden eagle of the legend was chosen as the national emblem of the Republic of Mexico.

Mexico's national emblem, the golden eagle, is portrayed on this coin, a silver peso.

# The Eagle in History

Countless legends, traditions, and religious beliefs revolve around the eagle. In Greek myths an eagle was a messenger for Zeus, and religious art often portrays an eagle with the Christian apostle John.

There is no truth to the legend that eagles attack unsuspecting humans or carry babies off to their nests.

Many armies were led into battle by eagle banners signifying the bravery, skill, and strength of the soldiers. Even knights of old, concealed behind their massive armor, were recognized by eagle emblems decorating their shields.

Eagle Coats of Arms

7

Eagle Talons
Used for
Spear
Ornaments

American Indians wore eagle feathers as badges of rank and courage. Twelve brown and white feathers from the tail of a young golden eagle would purchase an Indian pony. It was a sinful act for an Indian to kill the spirited eagle. In order to obtain the prized tail feathers, many tribes held eagles in captivity.

8

Osprey

Caracara

California Condor

Peregrine Falcon

Turkey Vulture

Barn Owl

Red-Tailed Hawk

## Birds of Prey

Eagles are known as raptors (rap-torz), or birds of prey. Other North American birds of prey are the night-flying owls and the day-flying hawks, falcons, ospreys, kites, caracaras (ka-ra-ka-ras), vultures, and condors. All predatory birds are carnivorous (kar-nih-vuh-ruhz), or meat-eating. They do not feed on plant food.

9

Everglade Kite

## Where Bald and Golden Eagles Live

About 59 species (spee-sheez) or types of eagles are found throughout the world. Only the bald eagle and golden eagle are found in the United States.

Bald eagles live near swamps, lakes, oceans, and river rapids. The northern race of bald eagles is larger than the southern race. In winter, northern bald eagles migrate south into portions of the United States. Southern bald eagles fly north into Canada during the summer. Today the bald eagle is rare throughout most of its range. Most reports of this eagle come from Florida and Alaska.

Golden eagles are found worldwide. They are birds of mountain cliffs, wide valleys, forests, and plains. Occasionally golden eagles are reported in the eastern United States, but they exist primarily in the wildest areas of the West.

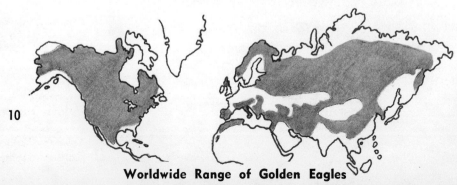

**Worldwide Range of Golden Eagles**

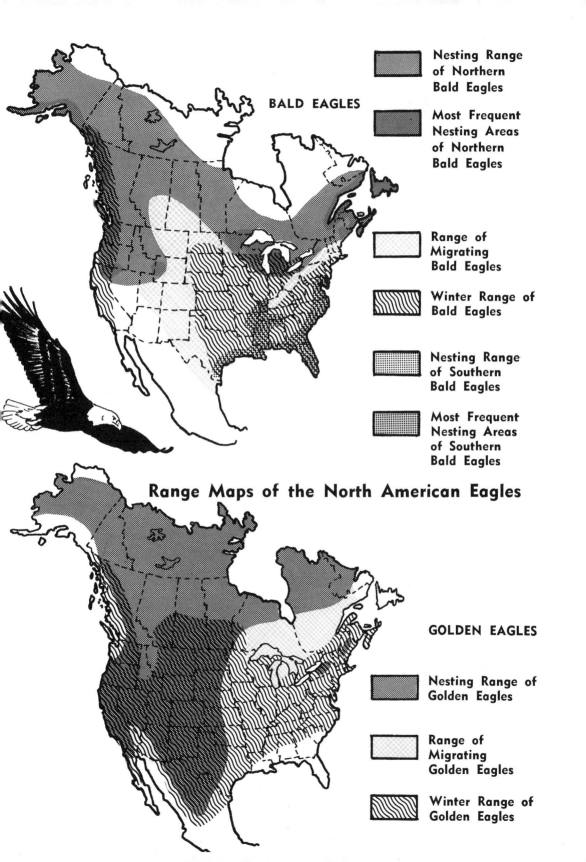

BALD EAGLES

Nesting Range of Northern Bald Eagles

Most Frequent Nesting Areas of Northern Bald Eagles

Range of Migrating Bald Eagles

Winter Range of Bald Eagles

Nesting Range of Southern Bald Eagles

Most Frequent Nesting Areas of Southern Bald Eagles

# Range Maps of the North American Eagles

GOLDEN EAGLES

Nesting Range of Golden Eagles

Range of Migrating Golden Eagles

Winter Range of Golden Eagles

Actual Size of Aluminum Ring
Used To Band an Eagle

Recovered bands are flattened and
returned to the government.

ADVISE FISH & WILDLIFE SERVICE
WASHINGTON. D. C.
509-21004

## Charles L. Broley (1880-1959), the Eagle Man

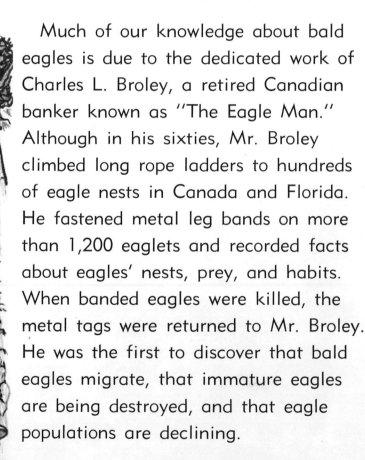

Much of our knowledge about bald eagles is due to the dedicated work of Charles L. Broley, a retired Canadian banker known as "The Eagle Man." Although in his sixties, Mr. Broley climbed long rope ladders to hundreds of eagle nests in Canada and Florida. He fastened metal leg bands on more than 1,200 eaglets and recorded facts about eagles' nests, prey, and habits. When banded eagles were killed, the metal tags were returned to Mr. Broley. He was the first to discover that bald eagles migrate, that immature eagles are being destroyed, and that eagle populations are declining.

12

The age of an eagle is determined by the number of years between banding and recovery. Records show that wild eagles may live for 20 years. In captivity, eagles have reached the age of 40.

## Naming Eagles

All over the world, scientists identify eagles by Latin names. If a bald eagle wore an identification tag, it would look like this:

**Class**—Aves (ay-veez), Latin word for birds

**Order**—Falconiformes (fal-kahn-ih-for-meez), "day-flying predatory birds"

**Scientific Family Name**—Accipitridae (ak-sih-pih-trih-dee), "the raptors"

**Genus (Scientific Describing Name)**—Haliaeetus leucocephalus (ha-lee-ee-tuz loo-koh-seh-fal-uhz), "white-headed sea eagle"

**Common Name**—Bald Eagle, American Eagle

The identification tag of a golden eagle would look like this:

**Class**—Aves

**Order**—Falconiformes

**Scientific Family Name**—Accipitridae

**Genus (Scientific Describing Name)**—Aquila chrysaetos (ak-wih-luh krih-say-tohz), "Eagle of Gold"

**Common Name**—Golden Eagle

13

**Immature Bald Eagle**

**Adult Bald Eagle**

When near its nest, the bald eagle screams a high-pitched squeaky cry—kweek-kuk-kuk.

**Pounds**

**Feet**
7
6
5
4
3
2
1
0

**Wingspan of Bald Eagle**

## Recognizing the Eagles

Long ago when the great American sea eagle was given its common name, the word "bald" meant "white." Its scientific name comes from the Greek word for white.

Like all sea eagles, the bald eagle has "short pants"—feathering only the upper portion of its legs. The adult bird has snow-white feathers on its head, neck, and tail which appear anytime after its fourth year. Immature bald eagles have mostly brown plumage. Except for their leg feathers, they resemble golden eagles.

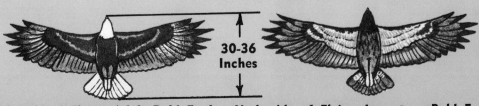

30-36 Inches

**Underside of Flying Adult Bald Eagle**    **Underside of Flying Immature Bald Eagle**

...ckles

Just before building their nests, golden eagles may call "kee-kee-kee."

**Adult Golden Eagle**

When an eagle is alert or annoyed, it fluffs out its hackles.

**Female**

White

**Male**

**Immature Golden Eagle**

Female eagles are always larger than their mates.

Land eagles, such as the golden eagle, are known as "booted" eagles. Their legs are feathered all the way down to their feet. The head and neck feathers, or hackles, of the majestic golden eagle are glistening golden-brown. Immature golden eagles have white tail feathers with dark brown tips and white patches on the undersides of their wings.

Feet

8
7
6
5
4
3
2
1
0

**Wingspan of Golden Eagle**

30-38 Inches

**Underside of Flying Adult Golden Eagle**     **Underside of Flying Immature Golden Eagle**

# The Eagle's Eyes

Long ago, people believed the fiery-eyed eagle stared directly into the sun until the searing heat and light renewed the great bird's strength and youth.

Eagles have the keenest vision of all creatures. An eagle can spot a possible meal from over two miles away. Even the moving shadow of a hidden animal attracts the alert bird's attention.

An eagle's eyes are located in the front of its face. The bird must move its head to direct its vision as the eyes rotate very little in their sockets. Once on target, the eagle's eyes never leave their goal, even when the bird twists its body, dives, tumbles, or brakes to stop.

The eagle has a special protective eyelid—the nictitating (nik-tih-tay-ting) membrane. This clear eyelid moves from side to side as it moistens the eye and shields it from harmful particles.

An eagle's eyes are located in the front of its face.

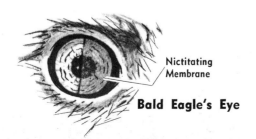

Nictitating Membrane

**Bald Eagle's Eye**

# Talons, the Eagle's Deadly Weapons

Black, razor-sharp talons, or claws, curve out from the eagle's three forward-pointing toes and single rear-pointing toe. These deadly weapons are used to seize, pierce, paralyze, and crush the eagle's victim in a viselike grip. A flying eagle carries its prey away in its talons. After landing, the eagle perches on one foot and uses the other to hold and move the object of food.

The eagle's scaled legs and feet indicate that birds and reptiles had the same prehistoric ancestors.

The undersurface of a bald eagle's foot is covered with small, thorny bumps, or spicules (<u>spik-yoolz</u>), which help it to grasp slippery fish-prey. Both bald and golden eagles have yellow feet.

The Scaled Leg and Foot of a Gila Monster (a Reptile)

The Scaled Leg and Foot of a Bald Eagle

Spicules

Talon

18

**Bald Eagle**

**Scimitar**

**Golden Eagle**

## A Beak for Carving

The powerful beak of an eagle resembles a curved oriental sword, or scimitar (sim-ih-tur). The fiercely hooked tip and sharp cutting edges enable the eagle to carve meat from animals it has taken for food. A golden eagle has a bluish-black beak with a yellow base. The immature bald eagle's black beak turns yellow as the bird reaches adulthood.

Predatory birds often "mantle" or cover their freshly killed prey before they eat it. Standing on the food object, they crouch over it with spread wings and tail.

19

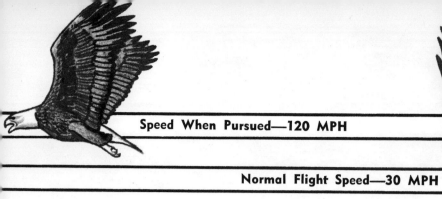

Speed When Pursued—120 MPH

Normal Flight Speed—30 MPH

With lightweight body and widespread wings, an eagle is able to soar hour after hour in graceful, undisturbed flight. Occasionally the eagle flaps a wing or tilts its tail to adjust speed or direction, but usually it rides on the wind currents like a floating glider far above the earth.

When hunting, the eagle suddenly hurtles toward its prey with wings partially folded. This diving plunge is known as a "stoop." When the eagle's tail and wings spread open to brake the impact, the talons strike their target.

Bald eagles often stoop to attack ospreys and rob them of their fish.

Speed of "Stoop"—175 MPH

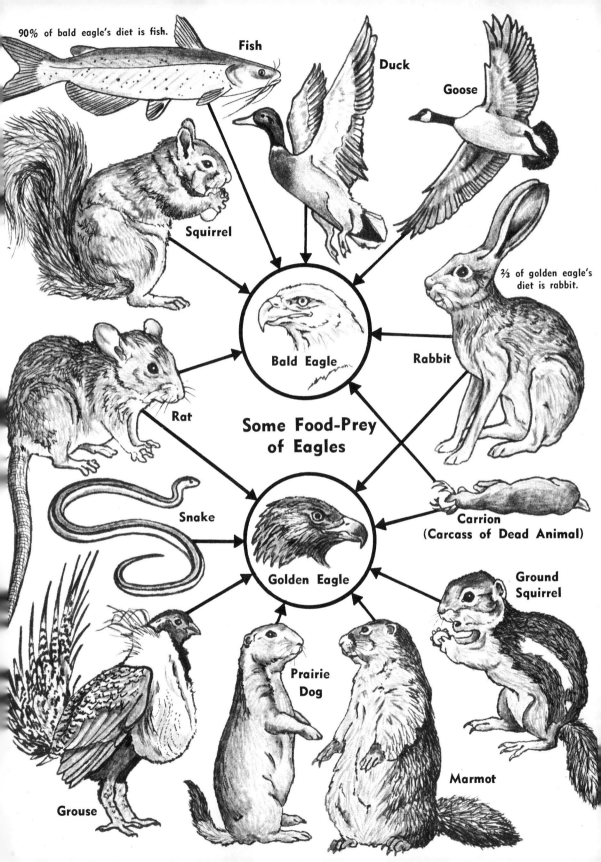

90% of bald eagle's diet is fish.

Fish

Duck

Goose

Squirrel

⅔ of golden eagle's diet is rabbit.

Bald Eagle

Rat

Rabbit

**Some Food-Prey of Eagles**

Snake

Golden Eagle

Carrion (Carcass of Dead Animal)

Ground Squirrel

Prairie Dog

Marmot

Grouse

# The Life History of Bald and Golden Eagles

When 4 or 5 years old, most eagles seek lifetime mates. The spectacular courtship flight is a breathtaking display of aerial acrobatics. Streaking past his chosen mate, the male eagle soars skyward, then plunges toward earth with half-closed wings. When it seems certain he will crash, the eagle opens his wings and shoots into the air to repeat his act and perform graceful loop-the-loops. The female soon joins him, and they fly higher and higher in ever smaller circles. Normally silent, courting golden eagles often call to each other in joyful mewing cries.

For a dramatic finale, bald eagles roll over in midair, lock their talons together, and spin through the sky like swiftly somersaulting pinwheels. Just above the ground the courting eagles break apart to climb skyward again. An eagle will only take a new mate if its partner should die.

Courtship Flight
of Bald Eagles

# The Eagle's Nest

**Golden Eagle Nest**

In the top of a towering evergreen tree close to water, mated bald eagles build their nest or eyrie (er-ee). Golden eagles usually build 2 or 3 eyries on ledges of steep-walled mountain cliffs.

Eagles return to the same nest year after year and add sticks, pine needles, moss, and any objects that attract them. Often they decorate their nests with green-leafed twigs or pine boughs. Nests 12 feet tall, 8 feet wide, and more than a ton in weight have been recorded.

In spring the northern bald eagle lays 2 or 3 eggs. The eggs of the southern bald eagle may be laid from early autumn through spring. Depending upon the climate, a golden eagle lays her 2 to 4 eggs anytime from February until June.

**Bald Eagle Nest**

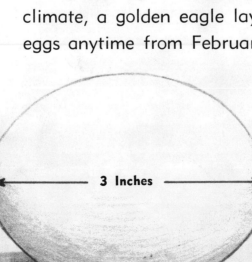

← 3 Inches →

Eagle eggs are kept warm by both parents. Bald eagles incubate their eggs for 35 to 38 days. Golden eagles incubate their eggs for 40 to 45 days.

**Actual Size of Average Egg Laid by Bald or Golden Eagle**

**Bald Eagle Chick, One Day Old (Actual Size)**

**4 Weeks Old**

**7 Weeks Old**

**10 Weeks Old**

A newborn eagle is helpless and unattractive. Its black eyes are open, and whitish-gray down covers its body. Usually the firstborn eagle is a male, while a female hatches a few days later. The stronger firstborn eagle attacks its frail new nestmate and may kill it. The parent eagles do not interfere. This brutal instinct is common among many bird species and is one of nature's cruelest mysteries. Perhaps when food is scarce this tragic act insures the survival of one strong eagle rather than two weak ones.

26

Adult eagles hunt constantly to provide food for the eaglets. At first the female parent carves bite-sized chunks of meat for her young. Eventually they learn to feed themselves on prey brought to the nest.

Golden
Eagle
Chick

2 Weeks Old

4 Weeks Old

7 Weeks Old

10 Weeks Old

After 9 weeks the eaglets have
developed their dark-brown juvenal
plumage. All day they preen their
feathers, stretch and flap their wings,
make mock attacks at their food, and
sleep. The young eagles are soon as big
as their parents and by their third month
have learned to fly. Until they master
the skills of hunting, immature eagles
stay with their parents. When the eagles
are 5 months old, they are on their
own—young rulers of the skies.

Golden eagles will not allow other eagles to
share their hunting territory which may cover
100 square miles, but bald eagles often feed in
large groups.

27

# Will the North American Eagles Survive?

In years past, men have dealt unfairly with the mighty eagles and caused their downfall:

1. BY SHOOTING golden and bald eagles accused of attacking livestock.
2. BY SHOOTING immature bald eagles which look like golden eagles or hawks.
3. BY PAYING BOUNTIES or rewards for dead eagles.
4. BY DESTROYING WILDERNESS NESTING AREAS for advancing civilization.
5. BY SPREADING POISONED BAIT for predators.
6. BY USING CHEMICAL PESTICIDES which cause eagles to lay thin-shelled or non-hatching eggs.

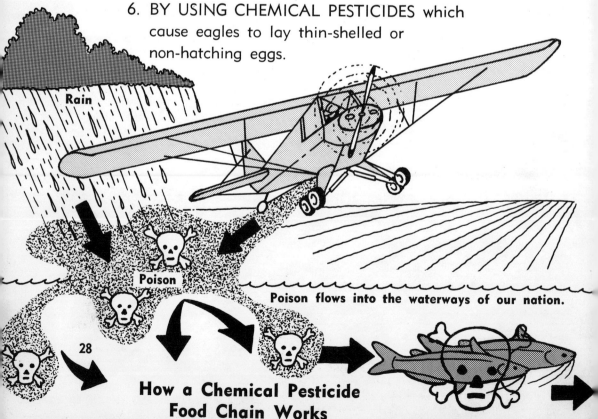

Rain

Poison

Poison flows into the waterways of our nation.

28

## How a Chemical Pesticide Food Chain Works

Today there is a federal fine up to 500 dollars or a 6-month jail sentence for harming a bald or golden eagle or for disturbing its nest, eggs, or eaglets. In addition, many state laws safeguard eagles.

In national forests and wildlife refuges eagles' nests are rigidly protected. More than 3 million acres of privately owned land in Florida have been set aside as sanctuaries for nesting bald eagles. Our government has wisely banned the use of the most harmful chemical pesticides, and 26,000 acres of public land in Idaho have been named The Snake River Birds of Prey Natural Area. This sanctuary protects the largest population of golden eagles in our nation.

In the United States, National Wildlife Refuges are marked with this sign of the flying Canada goose.

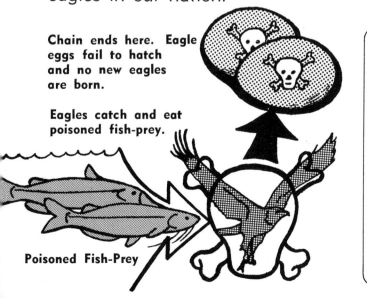

**Chain ends here. Eagle eggs fail to hatch and no new eagles are born.**

**Eagles catch and eat poisoned fish-prey.**

**Poisoned Fish-Prey**

# NATIONAL WILDLIFE REFUGE

U. S. DEPARTMENT OF THE INTERIOR
FISH AND WILDLIFE SERVICE
BUREAU OF
SPORT FISHERIES AND WILDLIFE

**UNAUTHORIZED ENTRY PROHIBITED**

1. If you know people who hunt, warn them not to shoot any large, soaring bird.

2. If you know people who use poisons in their gardens, ranches, or farms, tell them how poisons harm eagles and their eggs.

3. If you know where eagles are nesting, report it to a conservation organization. Then keep it a secret so no one goes near.

4. If you know people who say that eagles and other predators are bad, tell them what you have learned about eagles in this book.

5. Join groups to conserve, protect, and restore soil, water, air, plants, and animals.

6. Learn all that you can about nature, conservation, and endangered wildlife.

The bald eagle, our national emblem, is an endangered species. It could become extinct. The golden eagle is also threatened. The Birds of Freedom deserve your help.